A MODERN METHOD FOR GUITAR

by WILLIAM LEAVITT

VOLUME II

copyright 1968 BERKLEE PRESS PUBLICATIONS

1140 BOYLSTON STREET

BOSTON — MASSACHUSETTS — 02215 — U.S.A.

Introduction

This book is a continuation of Volume I, Modern Method for Guitar. Most of the terms and techniques are directly evolved from material presented there. For example, the entire fingerboard is covered at once in the five position C Major scale study. This is accomplished by connecting the four basic (types 1, 2, 3, 4) and one derivative (type 1A) fingering patterns that were, hopefully, mastered from the first book. (The sequence of fingering types will vary from position to position up the neck, depending upon the key.)

Study all material in sequence as I have tried to relate, as much as possible, all new techniques (physical and **theoretical**) to something already learned.

All music is again original and has been created especially for the presentation and perfection of the lesson material.

Please be advised that the pages devoted to theory are not intended to replace the serious study of this subject with a competent teacher, but only to, perhaps, intrigue the more inquisitive student and maybe shed some light into the mysterious workings of music for guitar players in general.

As before, good luck and have fun.

William G. Leavitt

It is important that the following material be covered in consecutive order. The index on page 117 is for reference purposes only and will prove valuable for review or concentration on specific techniques.

Outline
(Section I)

(Section II)

SECTION ONE
Four Basic Major Scale Fingering Patterns

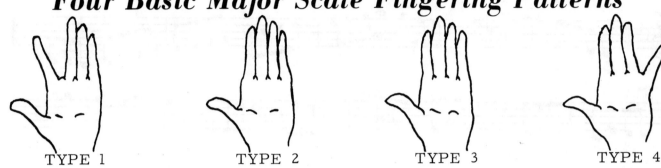

TYPE 1   TYPE 2   TYPE 3   TYPE 4

EXPLANATION: (S)= FINGER STRETCH... (REMEMBER DO NOT
MOVE ENTIRE HAND)

TYPE 1   ALL OUT OF POSITION SCALE TONES PLAYED WITH
FIRST FINGER STRETCHES. (SEE PAGE 60 VOL. I)

TYPE 2   NO FINGER STRETCHES NECESSARY FOR SCALE TONES

TYPE 3   NO STRETCHES

TYPE 4   ALL OUT OF POSITION SCALE TONES PLAYED WITH FOURTH FINGER
STRETCHES.

ALL SCALES (MAJ. and MIN etc.) WILL BE DERIVED FROM THESE FOUR
BASIC MAJOR SCALE FINGERING PATTERNS. ULTIMATELY 5 MAJOR KEYS
WILL BE POSSIBLE IN EACH POSITION WITH TYPE 1 AND ITS' FOUR DERIVA-
TIVE FINGERING PATTERNS - 1A, 1B, 1C, AND 1D. THIS SAME FACT APPLIES
TO TYPE 4 WITH ITS' DERIVATIVES 4A, 4B, 4C, AND 4D. FINGERING TYPES
2 AND 3 HAVE NO DERIVATIVE MAJ. FINGERING PATTERNS.

3

C MAJOR - ASCENDING - 5 POSITIONS

((S) = finger stretch)

C MAJOR - DESCENDING - 5 POSITIONS

Getting Up There (duet)

Moderately

Chord Etude No. 6

Mod. Slow

(Observe fingering carefully)

Melodic Rhythm Study No. 2

¢ = 2/2 HALF NOTE GETS ONE BEAT   2/4 QUARTER NOTE GETS ONE BEAT

(This is a notation comparison - Not a duet)

(¢ is referred to as "Alla Breve, Cut Time or In Two")

Triads (3 Note Chords)

CONSTRUCTION–from Major Scales....

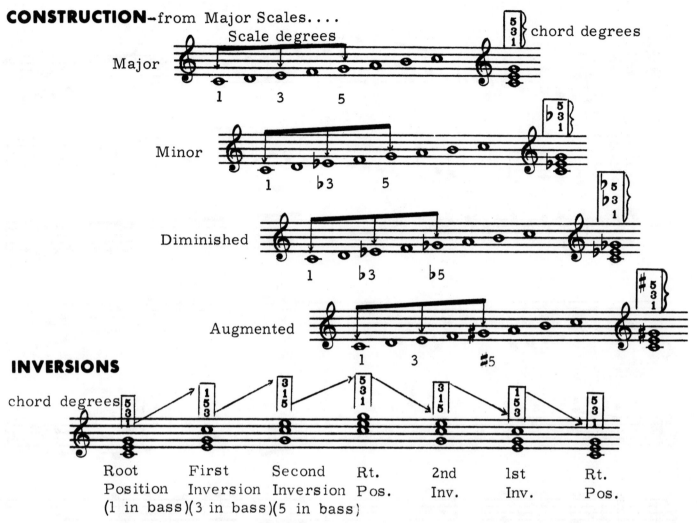

INVERSIONS

chord degrees

Root Position (1 in bass)	First Inversion (3 in bass)	Second Inversion (5 in bass)	Rt. Pos.	2nd Inv.	1st Inv.	Rt. Pos.

...PRACTICE THE FOLLOWING (ACROSS THE FINGERBOARD) C TRIADS.
MEMORIZE THE CHORD SPELLING AND FINGERING.....

NOTE COMMON FINGER and STRING RELATIONSHIPS BETWEEN MOST FORMS...

F MAJOR - ASCENDING - 5 POSITIONS

(F MAJ. ASCENDING)

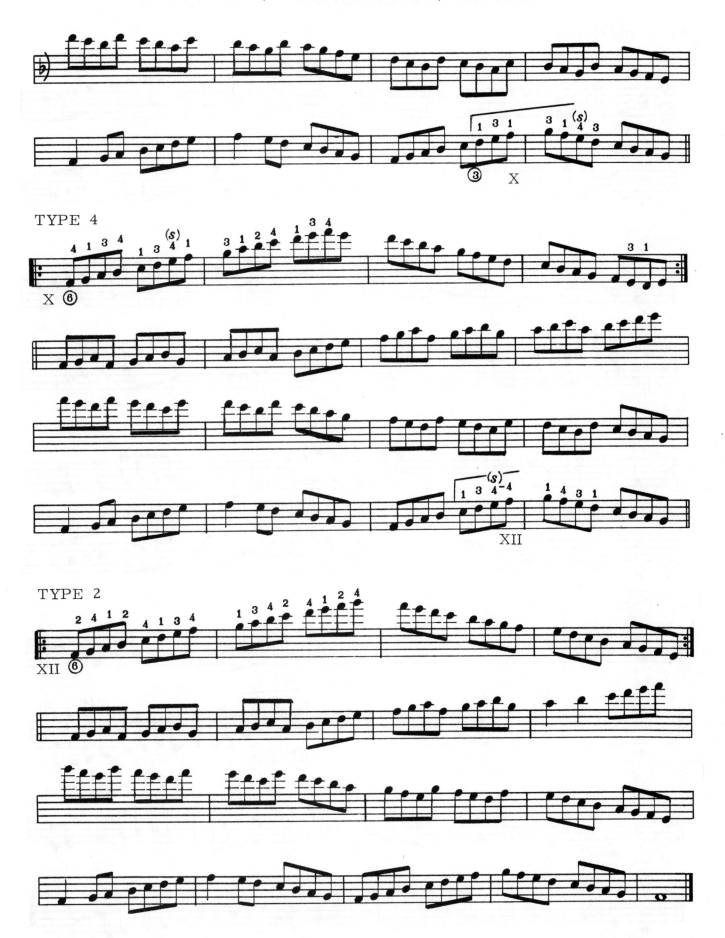

TYPE 4

TYPE 2

F MAJOR - DESCENDING - 5 POSITIONS

Another Waltz for Two (duet)

Chord Forms

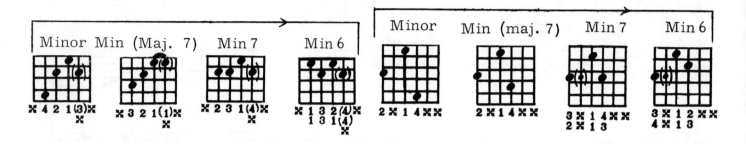

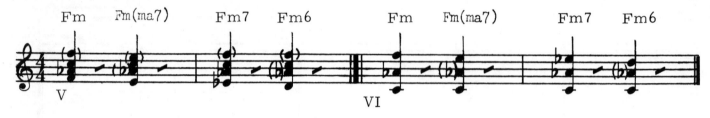

(ALSO SEE PG 121 - VOL I)

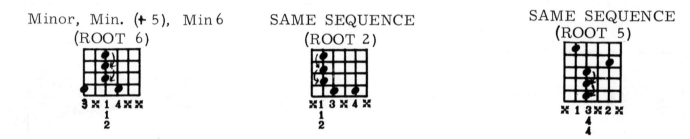

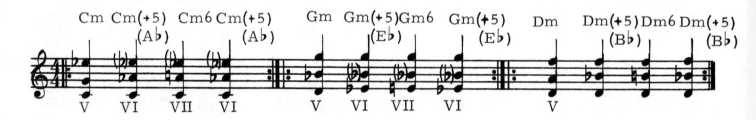

Speed Study

Keep tempo constant thru-out

14

(...FOR PRACTICE WITH OTHER FINGERING PATTERNS PLAY SPEED STUDY
AS WRITTEN BUT CHANGE THE KEY SIGNATURE TO A, D, G, AND C.)

Triads

(OBSERVE THE FINGERING - NOTE COMMON FINGER(S) BETWEEN MOST FORMS)

Rhythm Guitar - The Right Hand

FOR A GOOD RHYTHM SECTION BLEND, ALL NOTES OF A CHORD MUST SEEM TO EXPLODE INTO SOUND AT THE SAME INSTANT. THIS CAN BE ACCOMPLISHED BY A COMBINATION OF DOWNWARD, ROTARY FOREARM AND LOOSE WRIST MOTION, AS IF "FLECKING" SOMETHING FROM THE BACK OF YOUR HAND. THE PICK MUST TRAVEL VERY QUICKLY ACROSS THE STRINGS TO MATCH THE SOUND OF THE PRODUCTION OF A PIZZICATO NOTE ON THE BASS VIOL.

NOTATION: ⊓ = DOWNSTROKE   V = UPSTROKE

⌐ = STRIKE MUFFLED STRINGS - FINGERS IN FORMATION

, = RELEASE PRESSURE - IMMEDIATELY AFTER CHORD SOUNDS

(Note: All strokes labeled "Basic" are usually best when used with an incomplete rhythm section or guitar alone.)

BASIC STROKE FOUR, FOUR AND TWO BEAT   ORCHESTRAL FOUR, FOUR   THE "CHOP"

(often slightly amplified)

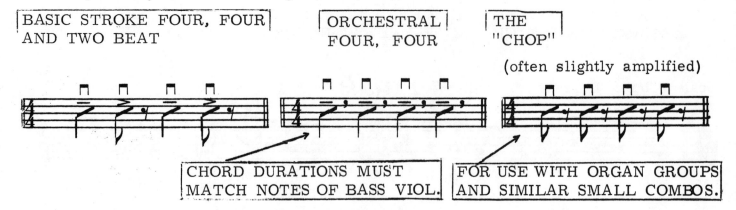

CHORD DURATIONS MUST MATCH NOTES OF BASS VIOL.   FOR USE WITH ORGAN GROUPS AND SIMILAR SMALL COMBOS.

Exercise (Practice in all 3 styles..with emphasis on the orchestral.)

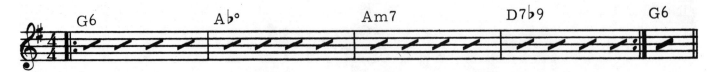

Note: The principal difficulty in the above orchestral stroke is in producing the sharp, explosive attack, while keeping the chord duration long.

ORCHESTRAL "TWO BEAT"

(*) It is sometimes advisable in practice (and in use) to lightly hit the (muffled) top strings on the returning upstroke where rests are indicated.

Exercise

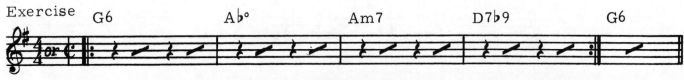

...Be sure to practice in slow, medium and fast tempos. When learning this style of rhythm playing it is necessary to tap the foot...first on beats 1 and 3..later on 1, 2, 3, 4.

16

| ORCHESTRAL FAST TO VERY FAST "FOUR" | | Tap the foot "in two" (i.e. on beats 1 and 3) |

Make the upstroke sound as much like the downstroke as possible by favoring the lower strings with the returning upstroke of the pick. There will be a slight natural accent on beats 2 and 4 because of the downstroke hitting the heavy strings first - but this is good, as it is comparable to the drummers use of the hi-hat cymbal on these beats.

Exercise

...This right hand technique is difficult to master, but it is extremely valuable for you can maintain very brite tempos (steady as a rock) with very little tightening up.

Chord Etude No. 7

3/8 Eighth note gets one beat

Moderately fast waltz   (All notes connected by curved line must be kept ringing)

G MAJOR - ASCENDING - 5 POSITIONS

(G Maj. Ascending)

TYPE 1

TYPE 4

G MAJOR - DESCENDING - 5 POSITIONS

Sea - See - Si (duet)

(TIME DURATIONS ARE RELATIVE - 16th NOTES ARE NOT ALWAYS VERY FAST)

Chord Forms

MOST OF THE CHORD FORM PAGES FROM HERE ON ARE HIGHLY CONCENTRATED. I RECOMMEND THAT YOU PRACTICE ONE LINE AT A TIME WHILE GOING ON WITH THE NOTE STUDIES ON THE FOLLOWING PAGES. KEEP COMING BACK PERIODICALLY UNTIL ALL FORMS AND SEQUENCES ARE MASTERED.

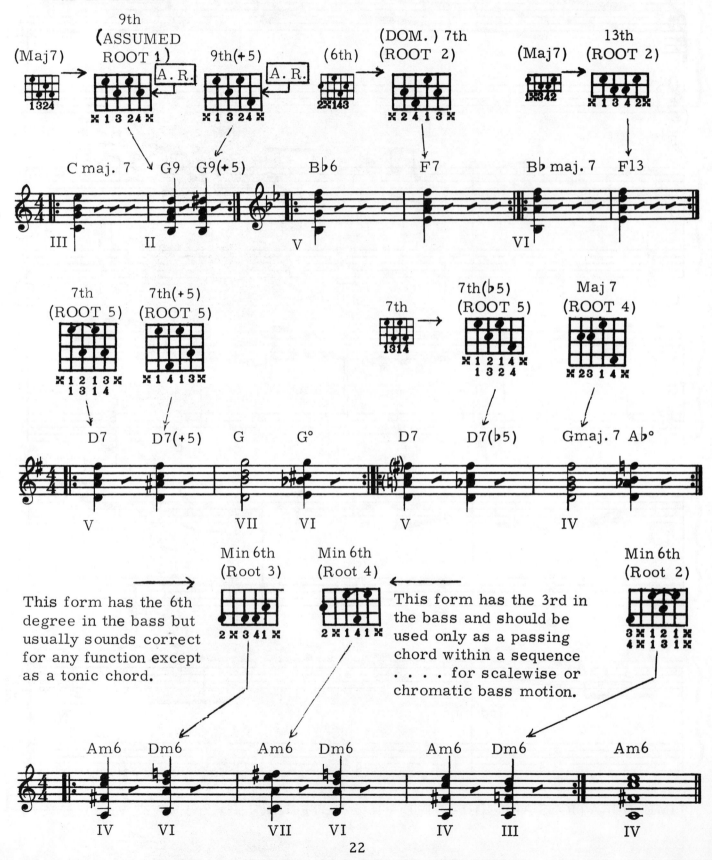

Triads

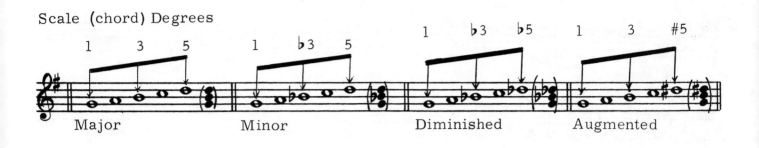

Scale (chord) Degrees

Major   Minor   Diminished   Augmented

(ACROSS THE FINGERBOARD..)

G Major

G Minor

G Diminished

G Augmented

Finger Stretching Exercises

D MAJOR - ASCENDING - 5 POSITIONS

FINGERING TYPE 3

TYPE 1

TYPE 4

TYPE 2

TYPE 1A

D MAJOR - DESCENDING - 5 POSITIONS

Melodic Rhythm Study No. 3 (duet)

Intervals

(Interval = the number of whole and half steps from one note to another)

1. Intervals (simple)

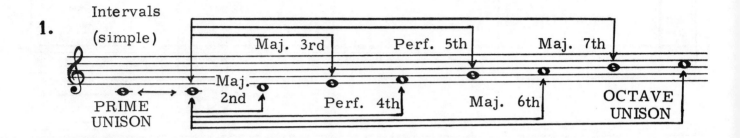

The above numbers represent the scale (and chord) degrees... and also the INTERVAL FROM THE TONIC.

(1) ...If the top note is a member of the MAJOR SCALE of the bottom note the interval is called... Major 2nd, Maj. 3rd, Maj. 6th, Maj. 7th or Perfect 4th, Perfect 5th, Perfect Octave.

(2)...Intervals one half step smaller than MAJOR are called MINOR. Intervals one half step smaller than PERFECT or a whole step smaller than MAJOR are called DIMINISHED. Any MAJOR or PERFECT interval expanded by one half step is called AUGMENTED.

2.

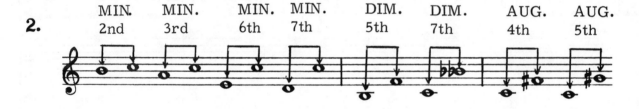

...When only the numerical term (a 3rd, 4th etc.) is used, MAJOR and PERFECT intervals are intended. MINOR, DIMINISHED and AUGMENTED intervals must be specifically named.

(3)...COMPOUND INTERVALS (larger than one octave) are described by the same terms as the SIMPLE INTERVALS (one octave or less) from which they are derived. (ex. Maj. and Min 2nd plus an octave = Maj. and Min 9th)

3. Intervals (Compound)

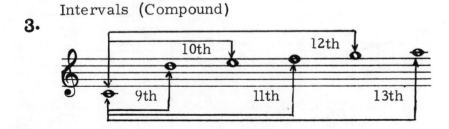

28

Triads

Scale (Chord) Degrees

(...ACROSS AND UP THE FINGERBOARD.. CAREFULLY OBSERVE
FINGERINGS AND STRINGS..)

29

A MAJOR - ASCENDING - 5 POSITIONS

Fingering Type 4

TYPE 2

TYPE 1A

(A Maj.-Ascending)

TYPE 3

IX

TYPE 1

XI

A MAJOR - DESCENDING - 5 POSITIONS

Chord Etude No. 8

Rhythm Guitar - The Right Hand

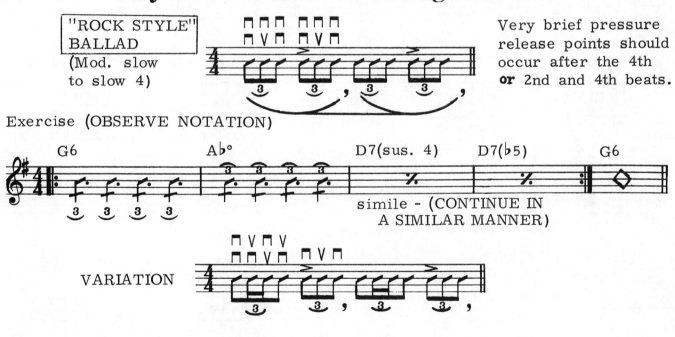

Note: These strokes are used with regular accoustic and amplified (high-register) rhythm playing.

Chord Forms

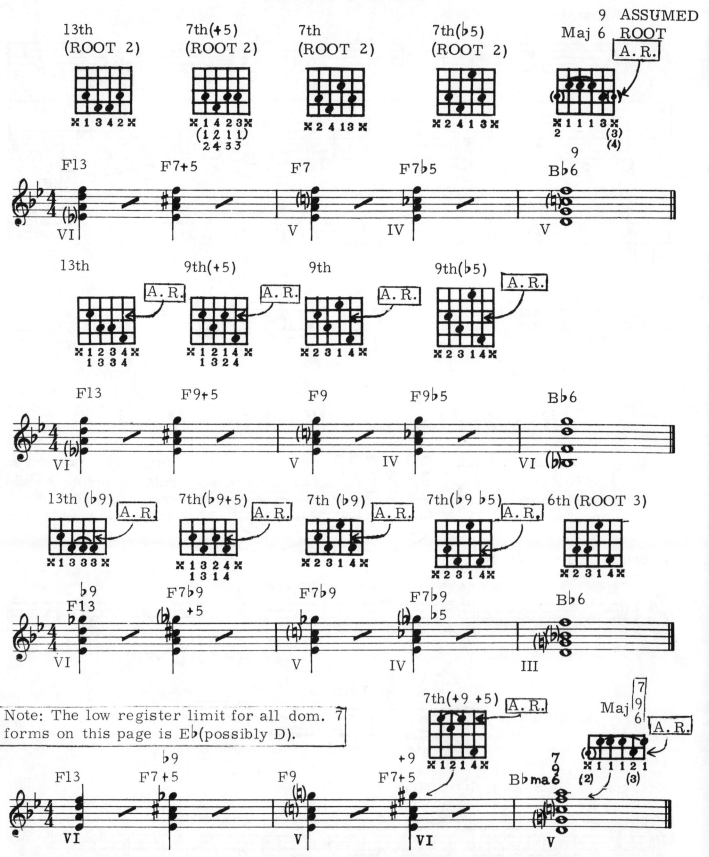

Note: The low register limit for all dom. 7 forms on this page is E♭ (possibly D).

DO NOT BE CONCERNED WITH THE THEORETICAL EXPLANATION OF THE MORE COMPLEX CHORDS - THIS WILL BE COVERED IN A LATER SECTION. MOST IMPORTANT FOR NOW IS THE PHYSICAL ABILITY TO PERFORM THEM AND EVENTUAL MEMORIZATION OF ALL FORMS, CHORD TYPES AND ROOT LOCATIONS.

NOTE THAT THESE ARE THE SAME FORMS AS THOSE SHOWN ON THE OPPOSITE PAGE. THE ROOTS ARE DIFFERENT AND THE ORDER OF SEQUENCE IS REVERSED. CONSIDERABLE TIME WILL BE REQUIRED TO REALLY LEARN THEM.

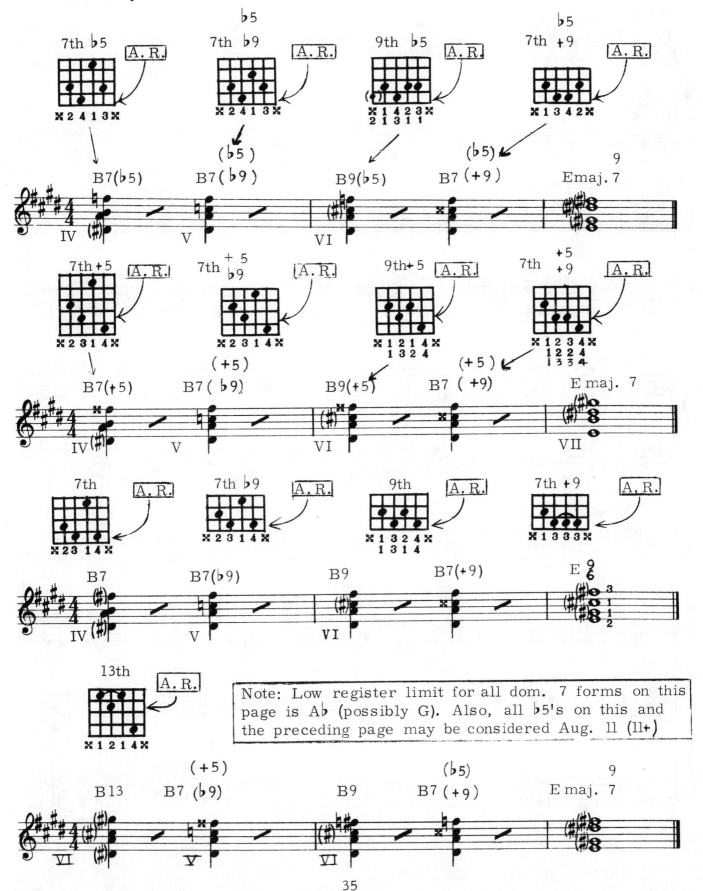

Tranquility (duet)

(SUSTAIN ALL NOTES FULL VALUE)

36

Triads

Scale (Chord) Degrees

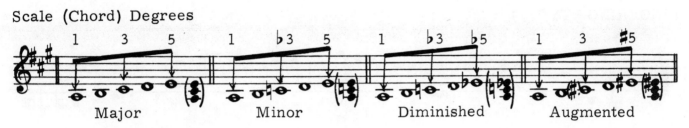

Major   Minor   Diminished   Augmented

(...ACROSS AND UP THE FINGERBOARD..CAREFULLY OBSERVE
FINGERINGS AND STRINGS..)

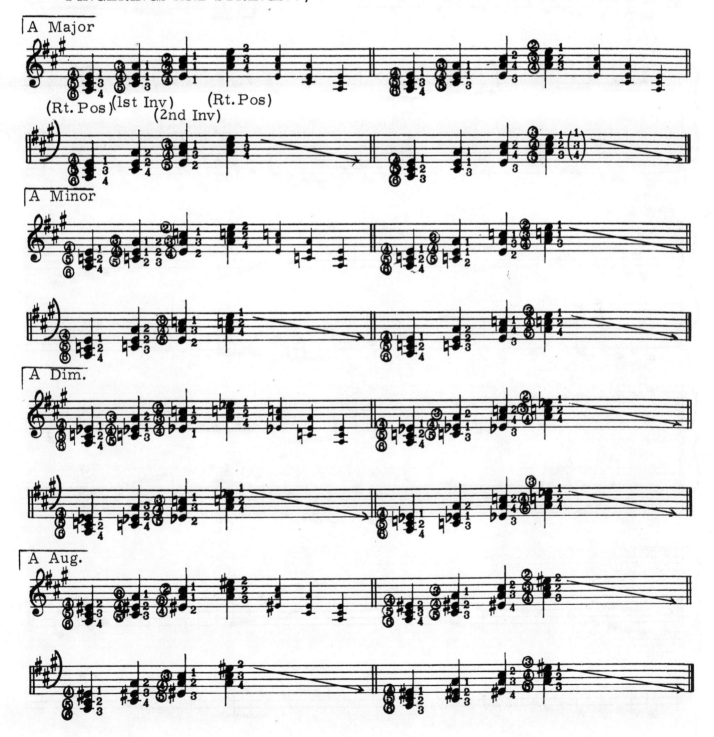

37

Bb MAJOR - ASCENDING -5 POSITIONS

FINGERING - TYPE 4

TYPE 2

TYPE 1A

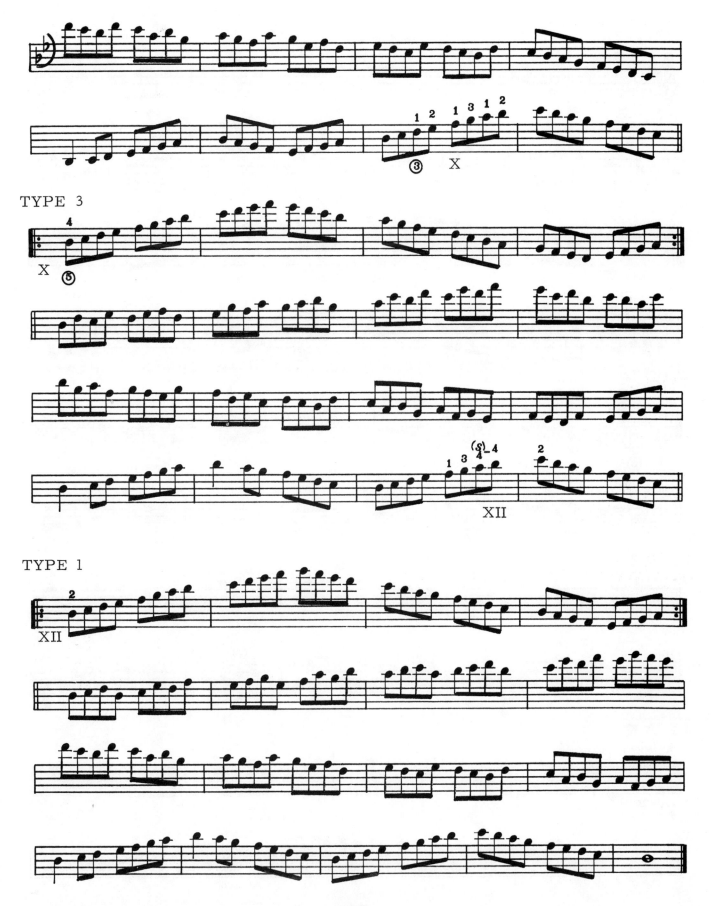

TYPE 3

TYPE 1

Bb MAJOR - DESCENDING - 5 POSITIONS

Fingering TYPE 1

TYPE 3

TYPE 1A

TYPE 2

TYPE 4

Waltz in Bb (duet)

Moderate Waltz Tempo

Melodic Rhythm Study No. 4

A FAST WALTZ IS OFTEN BEST COUNTED "IN ONE"... THE 2, 3 IS
MERELY FELT. SIX EIGHT IS USUALLY COUNTED "IN TWO"...
EACH MEASURE BEING DIVIDED IN HALF (LIKE 2 FAST WALTZ
MEASURES). HOWEVER A SLOWER 6/8 IS COUNTED 1-2-3-4-5-6..
(EACH 8TH NOTE GETTING ONE FULL BEAT.)

(This is a notation comparison – Not a duet)

(TIME DURATIONS ARE RELATIVE TO TEMPO AND TIME SIGNATURES)

Finger Stretching Exercises

Triads

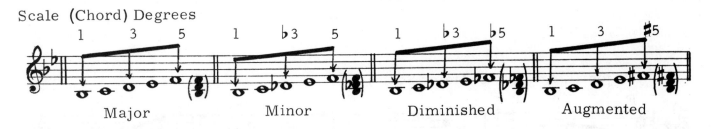

Scale (Chord) Degrees

1 3 5	1 ♭3 5	1 ♭3 ♭5	1 3 #5
Major	Minor	Diminished	Augmented

(...ACROSS AND UP THE FINGERBOARD...CAREFULLY OBSERVE
FINGERINGS AND STRINGS.)

43

Pentatonic (5 Note) Scales
(A GOOD PREPARATION FOR ARPEGGIO STUDIES)

Major (1, 2, 3, 5, 6, of Major Scale)

Tremolo Study
(QUICK REPETITION OF THE SAME NOTE)

At first practice very slow and even... Later gradually increase the
tempo, but keep it steady thru-out. Practice all "Loco" (in the same
octave as written) and also 8va (one octave higher than written.)

EXERCISE #1

(OBSERVE PICKING !)

ABBREVIATED NOTATION

EXERCISE #2

(OBSERVE PICKING !)

ABBREVIATED NOTATION

ABBR. NOT'N

ABBR. NOT'N

Eb MAJOR - ASCENDING - 5 POSITIONS

Fingering Type 3

TYPE 1

TYPE 4

(E♭ maj. -Ascending)

TYPE 2

TYPE 1A

Eb MAJOR - DESCENDING - 5 POSITIONS

BY TRANSPOSING THE PRECEDING 5 POSITION MAJOR SCALE STUDIES UP OR
DOWN ONE HALF STEP (ONE FRET, OR ONE POSITION) ALL MAJOR SCALES
ARE NOW POSSIBLE. EXAMPLE: D MAJ. POS. II TO Db MAJ. POS. I... Eb
MAJ. POS. III TO E MAJ. POS. IV
.....THESE SAME SEVEN (5 POSITION) STUDIES CAN BE USED FOR PRACTICE
IF YOU MERELY CHANGE THE KEY SIGNATURES AND POSITION MARKS.
....AS BEFORE ADDITIONAL READING MATERIAL MUST BE USED TO LEARN
THESE NEW KEYS.

Chord Forms

Major Scale Review - Positions II, III, V

(* v.s. means turn page)

* V.S.
(QUICKLY)

(Maj. Scale Review concluded)

THE CONSTRUCTION OF A MAJOR SCALE (UPWARDS) FROM ANY NOTE IS ACCOMPLISHED BY USING THE FOLLOWING SERIES OF WHOLE AND HALF STEP INTERVALS.

C D E F G A B C   F G A B♭ C D E F   G A B C D E F♯ G

OBSERVE THE HALF STEPS BETWEEN THE 3rd and 4th, 7th and 1st SCALE DEGREES IN ALL MAJOR SCALES. THE NECESSITY OF KEEPING THIS INTERVAL RELATIONSHIP ACCOUNTS FOR THE PRESENCE OF FLATS OR SHARPS IN THE VARIOUS KEYS.

52

Triads

Scale (Chord) Degrees

(...ACROSS AND UP THE FINGERBOARD...CAREFULLY
OBSERVE FINGERINGS AND STRINGS.)

Theory... Diatonic Triads (Major Keys)

(ALL NOTES BELONGING TO THE KEY SIGNATURE)

1.) There are 7 notes in every major scale and 7 chords common to each key. These diatonic chords **are** constructed upwards in thirds from each scale tone... and the structures (maj. min. dim. resulting from the scale) will be as follows in all major keys..

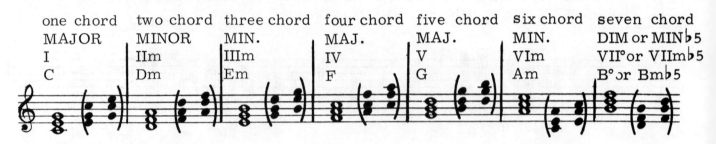

one chord	two chord	three chord	four chord	five chord	six chord	seven chord
MAJOR	MINOR	MIN.	MAJ.	MAJ.	MIN.	DIM or MIN♭5
I	IIm	IIIm	IV	V	VIm	VII° or VIIm♭5
C	Dm	Em	F	G	Am	B° or Bm♭5

Roman Numerals are used to represent these chord structures. (Be careful not to confuse them with position marks)... You must memorize the names and structures in all major keys.

2.) The principal chords and cadences (chord sequences) in maj. keys are:
   ..I V I called AUTHENTIC CADENCE..... C G C (key of C)
   ..I IV I called PLAGAL CADENCE ...... C F C (key of C)
   ..OR combined I IV V I (AUTHENTIC CADENCE)..C F G C (key of C)
In recent times the IIm chord has replaced IV in the preceding combined AUTHENTIC CADENCE....I IIm V I....C Dm G C (key of C)

3.) There are three basic chordal sounds in every major key that are represented by these diatonic chord structures, and the following specific terms are used to name them. "Tonic"≟ I chord, "subdominant"≟ IV chord, "dominant"≟ V chord. There are also names for the chords built on all other scale degrees but we will not discuss them here as they have no direct bearing on the (3) basic sounds, and they are usually referred to by number..i.e... the two (II) chord, the three (III) chord, the six (VI) chord, etc...

4.) The (7) chords in a major key are related to each other with regard to the three basic chordal sounds. The I, IIIm and VIm all produce a tonic sound. The IIm and IV chords produce a subdominant sound, and the V and VIIm ♭5 produce a dominant sound. These facts will be very important later on for chord substitutions and scale relationships in improvization.

	Tonic Sound			Sub-Dom. Sound		Dominant Sound	
Key of C	I	IIIm	VIm	IIm	IV	V	VIIm(♭5)
	C	Em	Am	Dm	F	G	Bm(♭5)

MEMORIZE CHORD NAMES AND (DIATONIC) STRUCTURES IN ALL MAJOR KEYS.

Diatonic Triads — KEY OF G MAJOR
Arpeggios and Scales

(Fingering Type 2)

(ALSO PLAY IN POS. IV, Fingering Type 1A)

KEY OF F MAJOR

(Fingering Type 3)

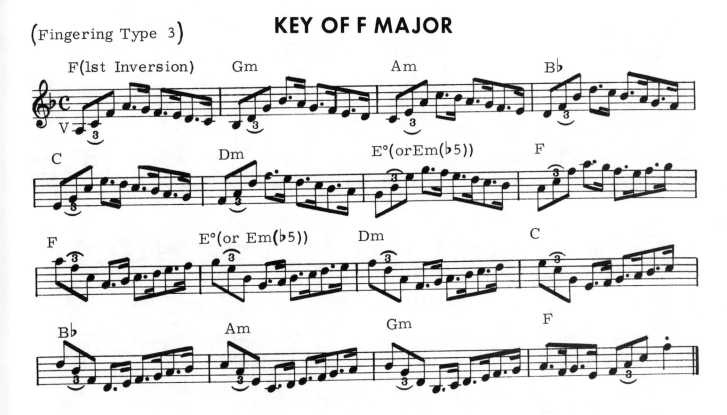

NOTE: WHEN TWO CONSECUTIVE NOTES ARE PLAYED BY THE SAME FIN-
GER ON ADJACENT STRINGS - "ROLL" THE FINGERTIP FROM ONE STRING
TO THE NEXT...DO NOT LIFT THE FINGER FROM THE STRING.

Diatonic Triads – KEY OF Bb MAJOR

(Fingering Type 4)   (Arpeggios and Scales)

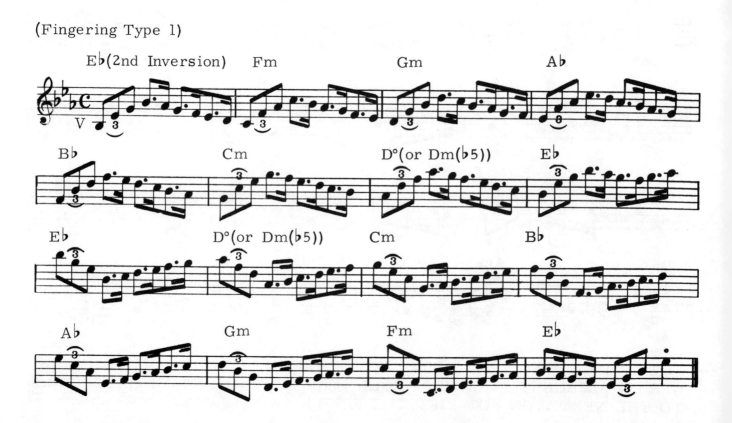

KEY OF Eb MAJOR

(Fingering Type 1)

5th Position Study (duet)

(Play ♪♪ as ♪♪)

MAJOR TRIADS EXERCISE ... up and down the fingerboard, thru-all
inversions on the same three strings...(Includes all 4 sets of 3
adjacent strings.)

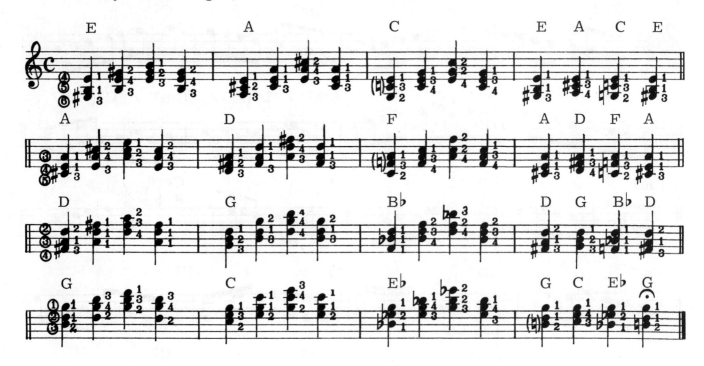

MINOR TRIADS EXERCISE .. up and down the fingerboard, thru-all
inversions on the same three strings...(Includes all 4 sets of 3
adjacent strings.)

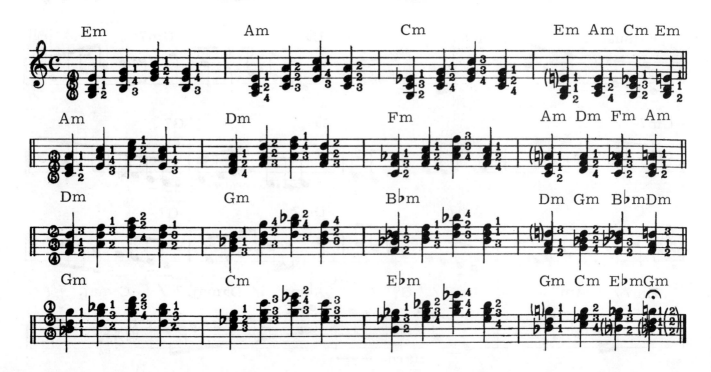

SECTION TWO

One Octave Arpeggios - Triads

(Fingering derived from scales - across the fingerboard.)

TRANSPOSE ON THE GUITAR, (BY MOVING UP THE FINGERBOARD, DO NOT WRITE OUT) AND PRACTICE THE PRECEDING ARPEGGIOS IN THE FOLLOWING KEYS.. A, B♭, C, D and E♭. ...ALL CHORD SPELLING MUST BE THOROUGHLY MEMORIZED.

GLISSANDO (gliss.)=Slide (same finger) from note to note

FAST SLIDE-
NOTES IN BETWEEN
MUST NOT BE
HEARD...

MORE DELIBERATE SLIDE-
NOTES IN BETWEEN ARE
VERY BRIEFLY HEARD....

Real Melodic or Jazz Minor Scale

The REAL MELODIC MINOR SCALE is derived from the preceding major scale forms by merely lowering the 3rd degree (note) one half step (1 fret). This is a tonic major to minor relationship. All notes in this melodic minor scale remain the same-ascending and descending.

In the real melodic (or jazz) minor studies on the following pages, tonic major key signatures are used to simplify the conversion from major to minor. All playing positions are exactly the same.

You must practice these minor scales carefully, as at first they are difficult to "hear". They are worth considerable effort as they play a very large part in improvisation. (Application will be discussed later.)

C REAL MELODIC MINOR - 5 POSITIONS

60

Rhythm Guitar - The Right Hand

SHUFFLE RHYTHM
BASIC STROKE

A very stable beat, but most practical with an incomplete rhythm section as all accents fall "on the beat."

Exercise (OBSERVE NOTATION)

Bm7　　E7♭9　　　Am7 /　D7♭9 /　G6

Similie

ORCHESTRAL
SHUFFLE
RHYTHM

Difficult to master... when learning, tap the foot "in four."

(Note: This stroke accents the "off beats" and therefore adds a great deal more to a rhythm section.)

Exercise (OBSERVE NOTATION)

G6　　　　　　D7(sus.4)　D7　　　　　G6

(...The preceding shuffle rhythm strokes also apply to rhythm parts in 6/8.)

Speed Study

TEMPO MUST BE CONSTANT THRU-OUT

(..For practice with other fingerings change the signature to C, F, D, and A.)

Chord Forms

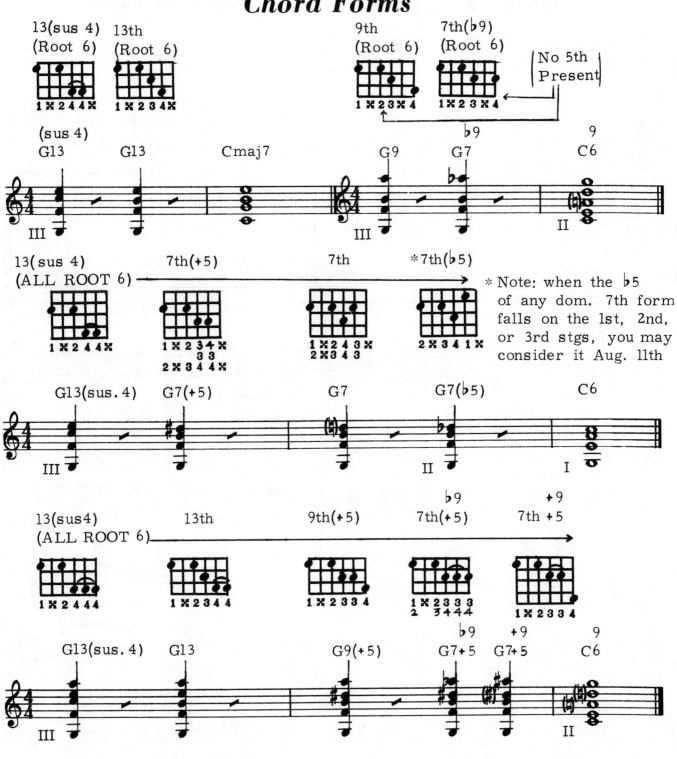

* Note: when the ♭5 of any dom. 7th form falls on the 1st, 2nd, or 3rd stgs, you may consider it Aug. 11th

Exercise-using some of the above forms... CAREFULLY OBSERVE the fingerings (and their relationships)...

Melodic Rhythm Study No. 5 (duet)

One Octave Arpeggios - Triads

(Fingering derived from scales - across the fingerboard.)

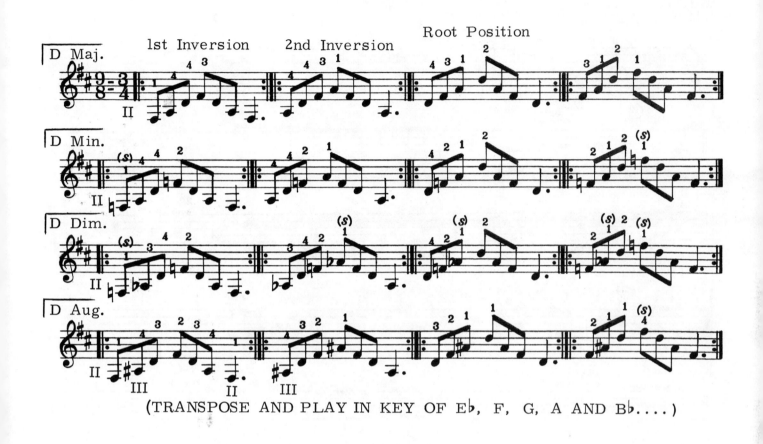

(TRANSPOSE AND PLAY IN KEY OF E♭, F, G, A AND B♭....)

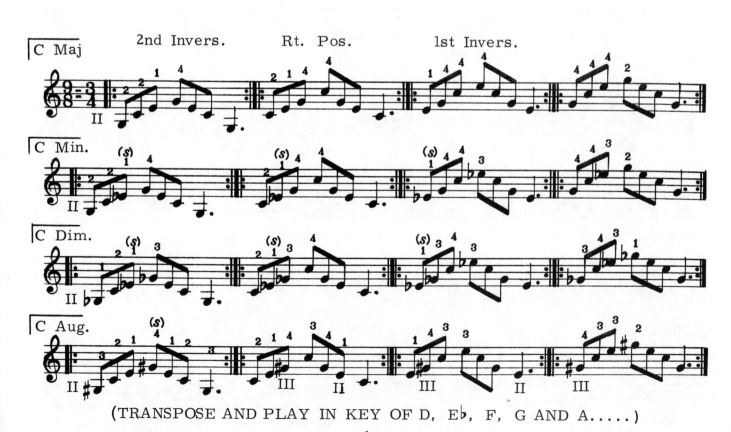

(TRANSPOSE AND PLAY IN KEY OF D, E♭, F, G AND A.....)

F REAL MELODIC MINOR - 5 POSITIONS

(F Mel. Min.)

FROM TYPE 2

For additional practice on real melodic minor scales refer to book I...play
reading and speed studies with lowered 3rd scale degree....

5th Position Study No. 2 (duet)

One Octave Arpeggios - Triads

(Fingering derived from scales - across the fingerboard.)

(TRANSPOSE AND PLAY IN KEY OF B♭, C, D, E♭, AND F.)

(FINGERING DERIVED ONLY PARTLY FROM SCALES...
ACROSS AND UP THE FINGERBOARD.)

(TRANSPOSE AND PLAY IN KEY OF G, A, B♭, C AND D.)

69

Chord Forms

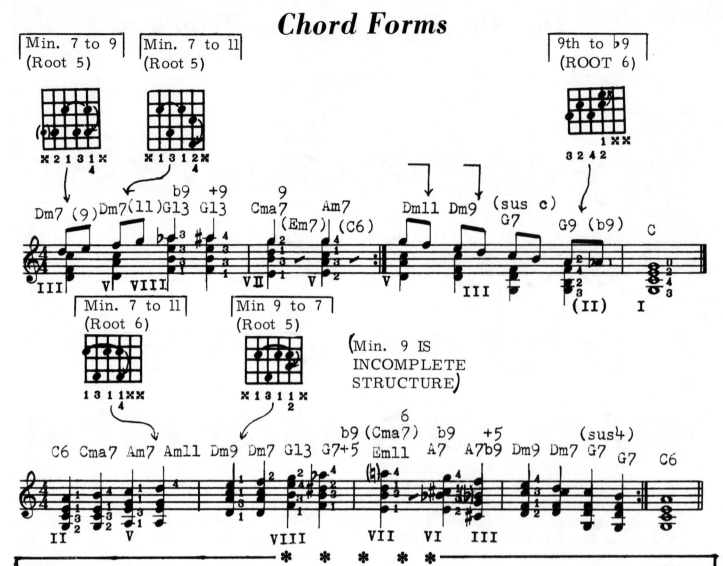

SLUR

ASCENDING...INDICATED BY A CURVED LINE OVER 2 OR MORE NOTES. PICK ONLY THE 1st NOTE AND DROP THE FINGER(S) OF THE LEFT HAND SHARPLY ON THE STRING TO PRODUCE THE REMAINING NOTE(S). DESCENDING..PREPARE THE ENTIRE GROUP OF NOTES WITH THE FINGERS OF THE L. H. IN PLACE. PICK ONLY THE 1st NOTE WITH THE R. H. REMOVE THE L. H. FINGERS FROM THE REMAINING NOTES OF THE SLUR, DRAWING THEM TOWARD THE PALM, SO AS TO ACTUALLY PICK THE STRING AGAIN.

WHEN BLENDING WITH HORNS (WITH ELEC. GTR) IT IS USUALLY BEST TO GLISS FROM NOTE TO NOTE WHEN A SLUR IS INDICATED...THIS PRODUCES NO ATTACK WHATSOEVER ON THE 2nd NOTE AND THEREFORE IS MORE "HORNLIKE". (NOTE: BE CAREFUL NOT TO MISTAKENLY INTERPRET A PHRASING MARK FOR A SLUR. A PHRASING MARK GENERALLY ENCOMPASSES A LARGE GROUP OF NOTES AND INDICATES A LEGATO OR SMOOTH PERFORMANCE OF THEM. YOU CAN ALSO EXPECT THE HORN PLAYER TO BREAK THE PHRASE OR BREATHE AT THE END OF A PHRASING MARK..FOR A PERFECT BLEND YOU MUST PERFORM ACCORDINGLY. (THE COMMA (,) IS ALSO USED TO INDICATE WHERE TO BREAK A PHRASE OR "BREATHE".)

TRILL

WHEN A GIVEN NOTE RAPIDLY ALTERNATES WITH THE NEXT DIATONIC
NOTE ABOVE IT...PICK ONLY THE PRINCIPAL NOTE..DROP THE FINGER FOR
THE NEXT NOTE SHARPLY ON THE (SAME) STRING..THEN DRAW IT OFF
TOWARD THE PALM, (ACTUALLY PICKING WITH THE L. H. FINGER) TO KEEP
THE STRING VIBRATING.

Theory... Diatonic 7th Chords (Major Keys)

(ALL DIATONIC CHORDS WITHIN A KEY ARE BUILT UPWARDS IN 3rds)

1.) BY ADDING ANOTHER NOTE A 3rd ABOVE THE DIATONIC TRIADS WE CON-
STRUCT ALL FOUR PART CHORDS COMMON TO A MAJOR KEY. (SEE DIAT.
TRIADS, PG. 54)

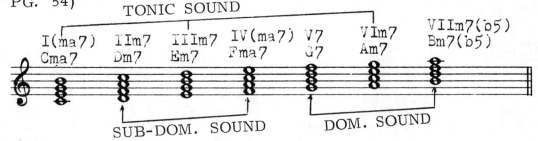

NOTE: THE VIIm7♭5 IS SOMETIMES CALLED "HALF DIMINISHED".. (SYMBOL = ⌀)

........OBSERVE THE CHORD RELATIONSHIPS PRODUCING THE TONIC,
SUB-DOM. AND DOM. SOUNDS.

ALSO NOTE: THE IIIm7 IS OFTEN FOUND AS AN INTERMEDIATE CHORD IN A
SUBDOMINANT SEQUENCE.. EXAMPLES:

| IV | IIIm7 | IIm7 | (V7 | I)... | IIm7 | IIIm7 | IV | (V7 | I) |
| Fma7 | Em7 | Dm7 | (G7 | Cma7).. | Dm7 | Em7 | Fma7 | (G7 | Cma7) |

2.) BECAUSE OF A CONFLICT WITH THE ROOT IN THE MELODY, THE FOUR
PART STRUCTURES USED ON THE ONE (1) AND FOUR (4) ARE OFTEN 6th
CHORDS..BUILT FROM MAJOR SCALE DEGREES 1, 3, 5, 6 YOU MIGHT SAY THIS
IS A RESULT OF THE SUBSTITUTION OF VIm7 OVER THE ROOT OF THE ONE
CHORD AND IIm7 OVER THE ROOT OF THE IV CHORD..(Am7=C6 / Dm7=F6)

3.) SUBSTITUTION OF IIIm7 OR VIm7 FOR I, IIm7 FOR IV AND VIIm7♭5 FOR
V7 ARE ESPECIALLY VALUABLE WHEN CREATING MOVING BASS LINES WITH
STRONG CHORDAL DEGREES (1 & 5) SUPPORTING THE HARMONIC STRUCTURES.

EXAMPLE:

All diatonic chords (names and structures) must be memorized, in all keys...

Arpeggios-Diatonic Sevenths

(ALL 4 PART CHORDS-ALL INVERSIONS-KEY OF G MAJ.)

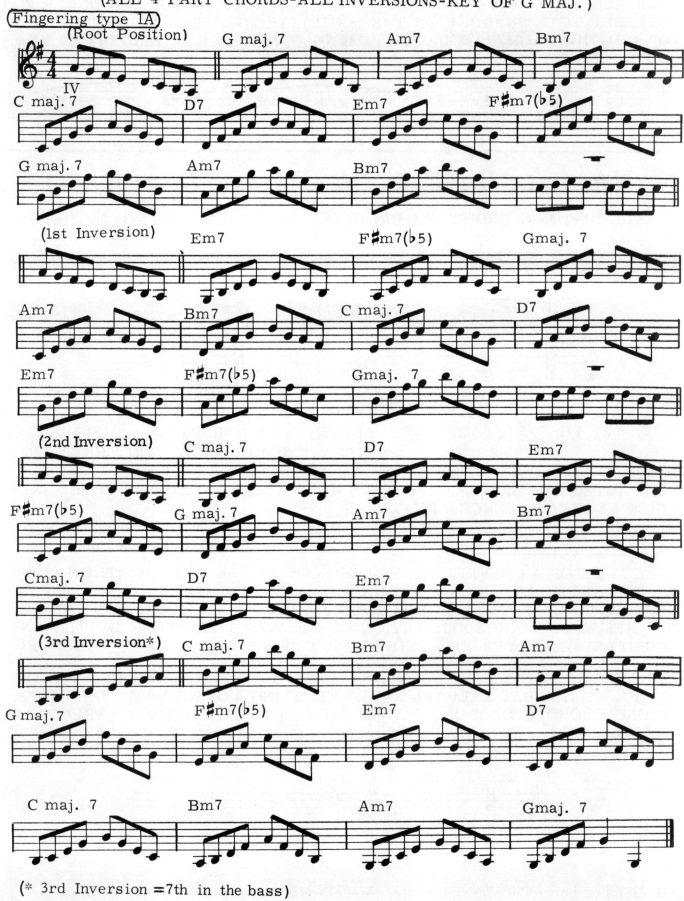

(* 3rd Inversion = 7th in the bass)

Arpeggios-Diatonic Sevenths

(ALL 4 PART CHORDS - ALL INVERSIONS - KEY OF C MAJ.)

Fingering type 4

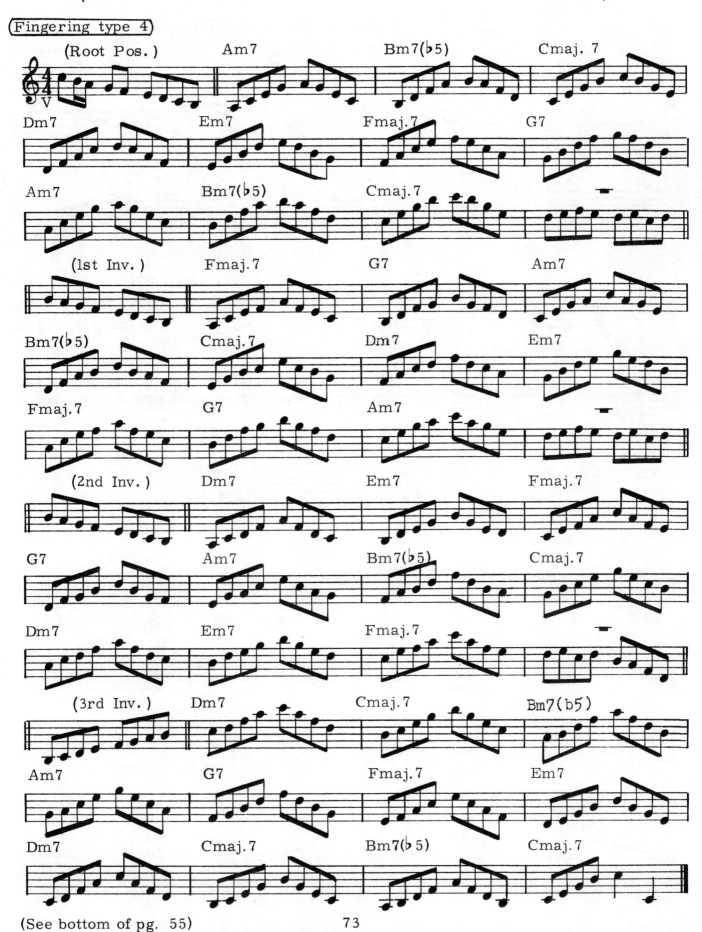

(See bottom of pg. 55)   73

G REAL MELODIC MINOR - 5 POSITIONS

(G Mel. Min.)

FROM TYPE 4

75

Chord Forms

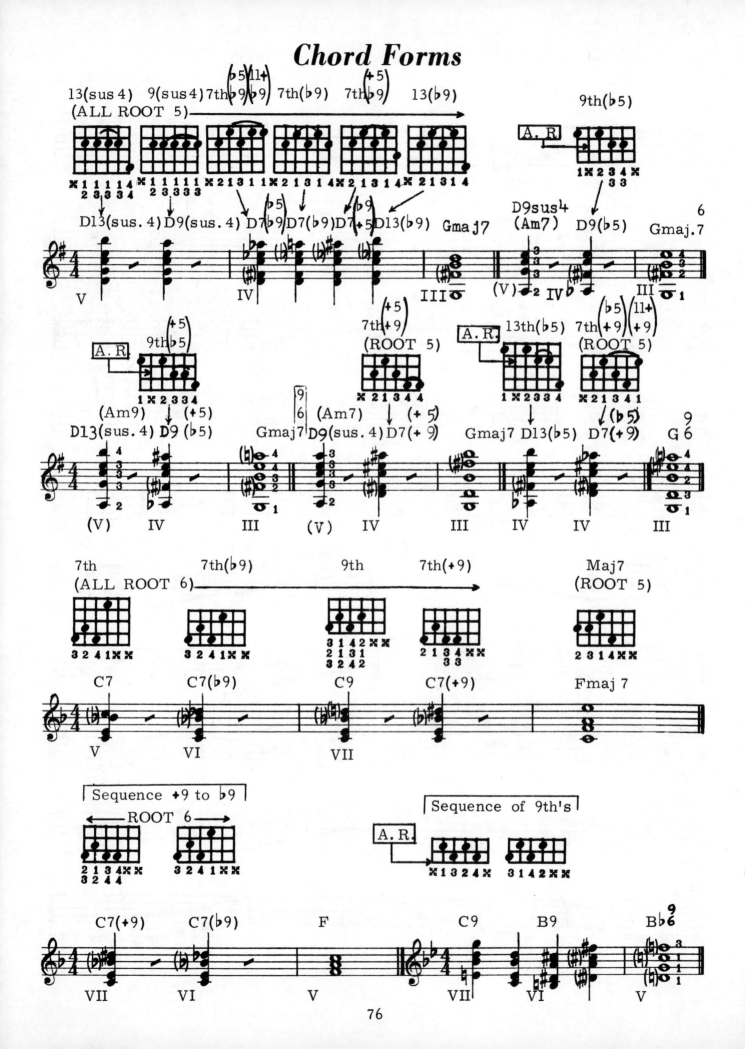

76

Two Octave Arpeggios

C MAJOR TRIAD FROM THE ROOT

(Fingering derived from scales and chords...Across and up the fingerboard.)

(PRACTICE ALL FORMS IN ALL POSSIBLE KEYS...)

Chord Etude No. 9

The Wanderer (duet)

Moderately Slow

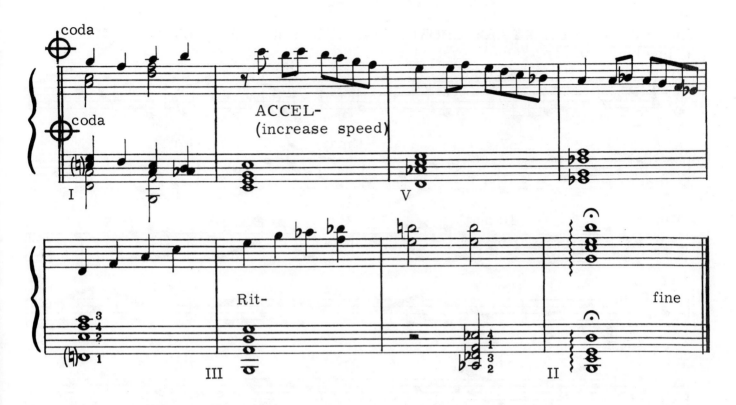

Rhythm Guitar - The Right Hand

Arpeggios-Diatonic Seventh's

(ALL 4 PART CHORDS - ALL INVERSIONS - KEY OF F MAJ.)

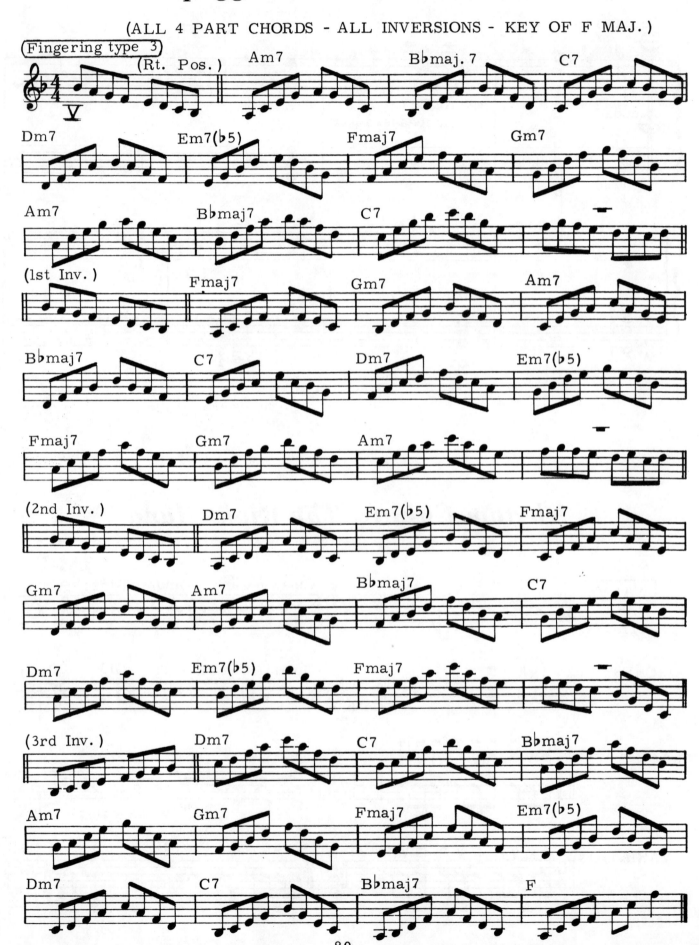

Theory... Chord - Scale Relationships

(FOR THE PURPOSE OF IMPROVISATION*)

WITH DIATONIC CHORD STRUCTURES

ALL THE NOTES OF A MAJOR SCALE MAY BE USED MELODICALLY OVER THE SEVEN CHORD STRUCTURES CONTAINED IN THAT KEY...HOWEVER, ANY SCALE TONE ONE HALF STEP ABOVE A CHORD TONE (1, 3, 5, 7 IN DIATONIC HARMONY) MUST BE OF SHORT DURATION AND USED ONLY IN "PASSING" TO A CHORD TONE NEXT TO IT.

EXAMPLE:

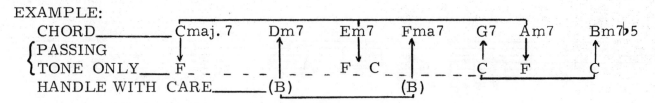

(..MELODIC IDEAS MAY BE CREATED FROM SCALE TONES IN ANY ORDER PROVIDING YOU DO NOT START WITH, OR "LEAN ON" THE PASSING TONES DISCUSSED ABOVE.

*IMPROVIZATION = THE SPONTANEOUS CREATION OF MUSIC WHILE PLAYING___ USUALLY WITHIN THE CONFINES OF THE HARMONIC CONTENT OF A SONG. (WITH ALL AVAILABLE NOTES DRAWN FROM CHORD TONES AND RELATED SCALES.)

BEFORE "ALL OUT" (NO HOLDS BARRED) IMPROVIZATION IS ATTEMPTED ON THE CHORDS TO A SONG, IT IS BEST IF YOU "STAY CLOSE TO THE MELODY" AND "FILL IN" ONLY DURING NOTES OF LONG DURATION.

Example:

(STRAIGHT MELODY)

(WITH "FILLS" AND SLIGHT RHYTHMIC VARIATIONS ON THE MELODY)

D REAL MELODIC MINOR - 5 POSITIONS

FINGERING DERIVED
FROM TYPE 3

FROM TYPE 1

FROM TYPE 4

FROM TYPE 2

(D Melodic Minor)

FROM TYPE 1A

fine

Chord Forms - 3rd in the Bass*

* ANY NOTE FROM APPROXIMATELY C, 5th STRING (3rd FRET) OR C, 6th STG..(8th FRET) ON DOWN IN PITCH I DEFINE AS THE REAL BASS (SOUNDING) RANGE.

....ANY CHORD VOICED WITH THE 3rd DEGREE IN THE BASS HAS A WEAK CHORDAL SOUND, AND SHOULD BE USED ONLY WHEN LEAPING TO A NEW INVERSION OF THE SAME CHORD..OR AS A "PASSING CHORD" TO PRODUCE SCALEWISE OR CHROMATIC BASS MOTION.

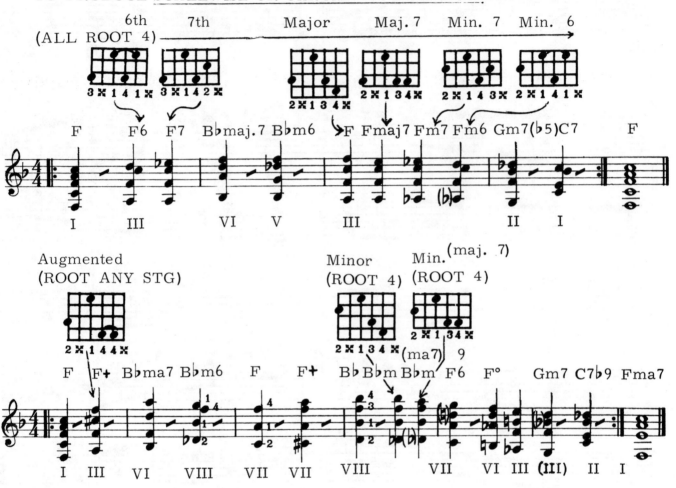

Chord Etude No. 10

Rubato

84

Two Octave Arpeggios

G MAJOR TRIAD FROM THE 3rd

(Fingering derived from scales and chords...Across and up the fingerboard.)

(Practice all forms in all possible keys..)

F MAJOR TRIAD FROM THE 5th (Across and up the fingerboard.)

(Practice all forms in all possible keys..)

Rhythm Guitar - The Right Hand

JAZZ WALTZ
BASIC STROKE

(⊠) → (bass note or muffled bass stgs)

ORCHESTRAL #1

(Tap the foot in "one".. i.e. on the first beat of each measure.)

VARIATION

COMBINATION

ORCHESTRAL #2

(Tap the foot in "one")

VARIATION

COMBINATION

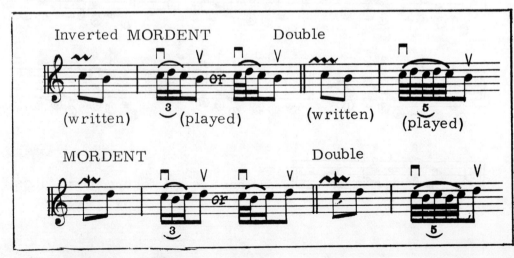

Inverted MORDENT   Double

(written)   (played)   (written)   (played)

MORDENT   Double

Arpeggios-Diatonic Seventh's

(ALL 4 PART CHORDS - ALL INVERSIONS - KEY OF B♭ MAJOR)

A REAL MELODIC MINOR - 5 POSITIONS

FINGERING DERIVED
FROM TYPE 4

FROM TYPE 2

FROM TYPE 1A

FROM TYPE 3

(A Mel. Min.)

FROM TYPE 1

Chord Forms

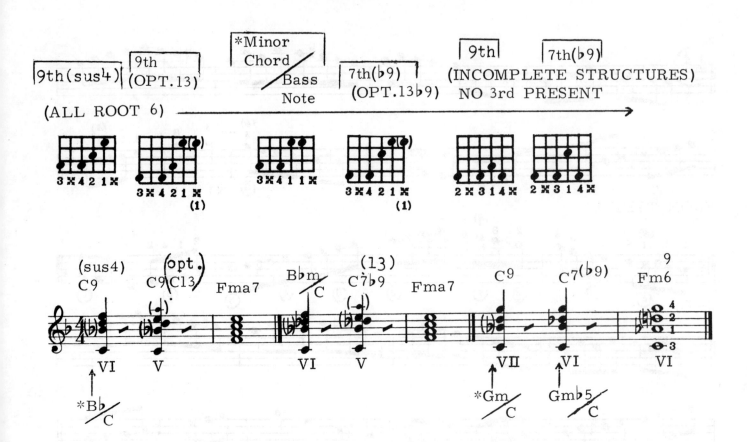

*This is a relatively new way of notating symbols for chord structures that might be difficult to name any other way. The basic chord sound is represented above the diagonal line, the bass note it is to be placed over is indicated below it.

Two Octave Arpeggios – C MINOR TRIAD FROM THE ROOT

(Fingering derived from scales and chords...Across and up the fingerboard.)

(Practice all forms

in all possible keys)

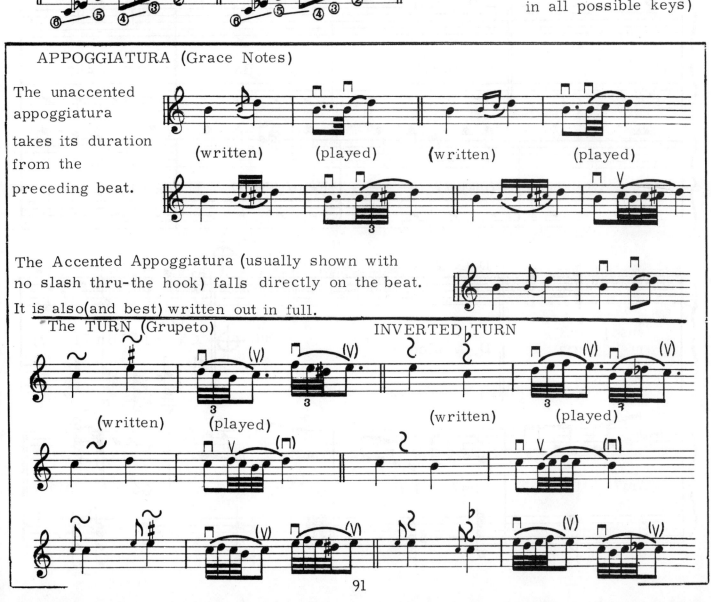

APPOGGIATURA (Grace Notes)

The unaccented
appoggiatura
takes its duration
from the
preceding beat.

(written)   (played)   (written)   (played)

The Accented Appoggiatura (usually shown with
no slash thru-the hook) falls directly on the beat.

It is also(and best) written out in full.

The TURN (Grupeto)   INVERTED TURN

(written)   (played)   (written)   (played)

Melodic Rhythm Study No. 6 duet

Rhythm Guitar - The Right Hand

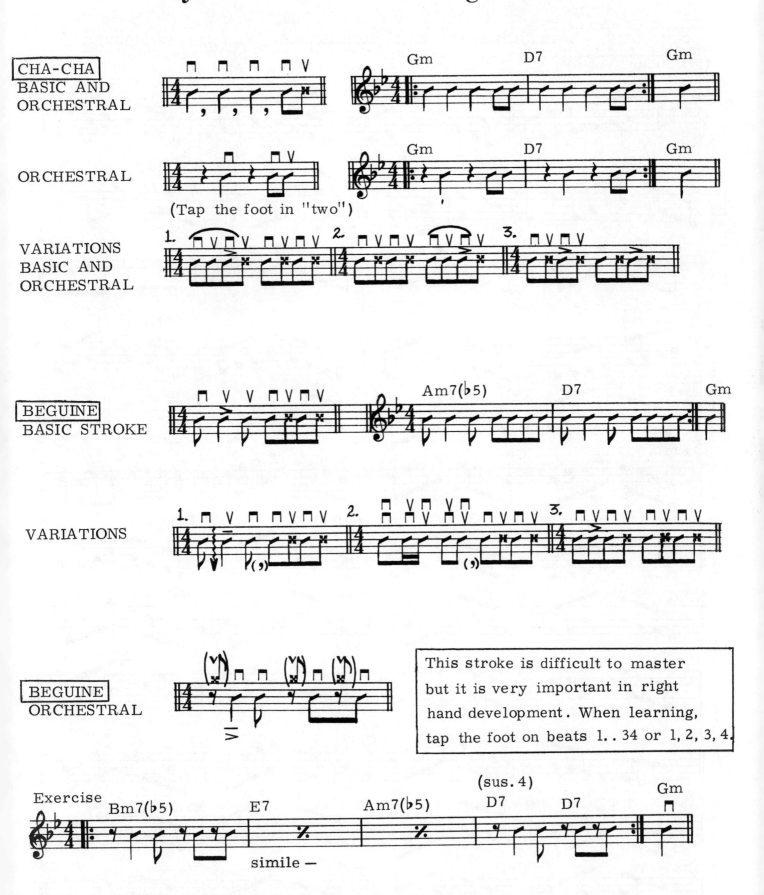

This stroke is difficult to master but it is very important in right hand development. When learning, tap the foot on beats 1..34 or 1, 2, 3, 4.

93

Arpeggios-Diatonic Seventh's

(ALL 4 PART CHORDS - ALL INVERSIONS - KEY OF Eb MAJ.)

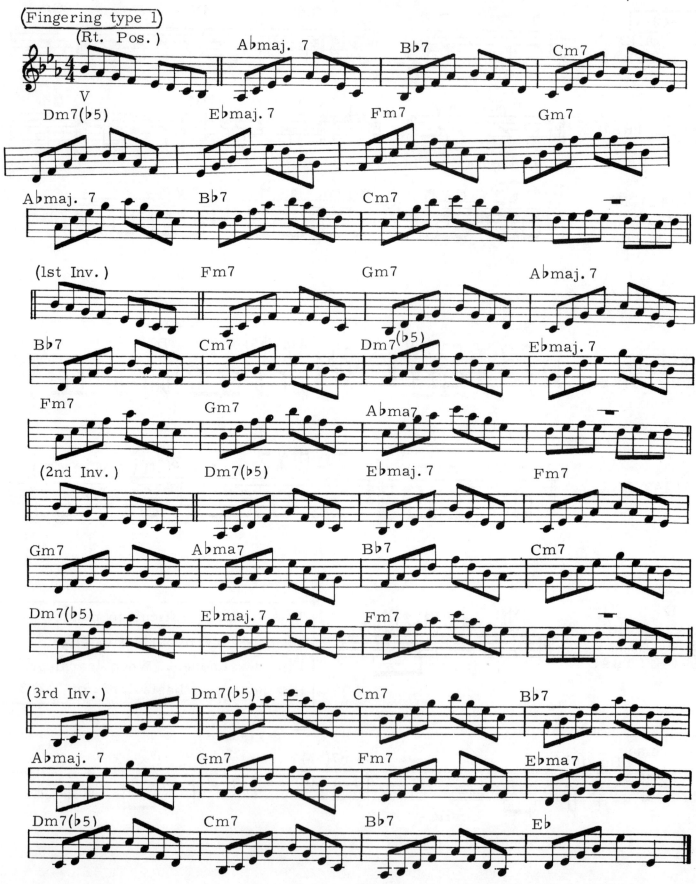

Theory... Chord - Scale Relationships
(FOR THE PURPOSE OF IMPROVIZATION)

...It is very rare when a song remains completely diatonic harmonically, from beginning to end.

...Any chord that does not conform to the diatonic structures actually is a modulation to another key (or scale) for its' duration.

...Sometimes a series of non-diatonic chords completely changes the key for a period of time. (This is why there will be references to "the key of the moment" in some of the following discussions on chord-scale relationships.)

...Because the melody usually remains reasonably diatonic thru-out a song, the ear, almost always, wishes to return to the original tonality.

...Also, and remember this, "the ear has memory but no eyes"...therefore the sound of what has gone on before has a definite influence on which scales belong to certain chords in particular situations..(but what is yet to sound has no bearing whatsoever.)

NON - DIATONIC MINOR 7 AND MAJOR CHORDS

1.) Any minor 7th chord not in the key (of the moment) usually wants to sound like a IIm7...of whatever key it is the 2nd diatonic structure. (..a non-diatonic min. 7th chord actually performs the function of *modulation more thoroughly than dom 7th chords.) Use major scale from one whole step below chord name for non-diat. min 7th.

EXAMPLE:

CHORD -	C	Cm7	Dm7	G7	Ebm7	Ab7	Abm7	Db7	C
SCALE -	Cmaj.	Bbmaj	Cmaj	→	Dbmaj	→	Gbmaj	→	Cmaj

(* Modulation - the change of key within a composition or arrangement)

2.) Any major chord not in the key (of the moment)..not preceded by modulation, with a non-diatonic root wants to sound like a IV chord...of what ever key it is the 4th diatonic structure.-Use major scale from 5th chordal degree of maj. chord with non-diat. root.

EXAMPLE:

CHORD –	C	Eb(ma7)	Dm7	G7	Ab(ma7)	Db(ma7)	C
SCALE –	Cmaj	Bbmaj	Cmaj	→	Ebmaj	Abmaj	Cmaj

3.) Any major chord not in the key (of the moment)..not preceded by modulation, with a scale tone root usually wants to sound like a one (tonic) chord. Use major scale from chord name of non-diatonic major chord with scale tone Root.

EXAMPLE:

CHORD ——	C	E(ma7)	G9susC	G7	C
SCALE ——	Cmaj	Emaj	Cmaj	→	→

(Note: The major scale constructed from the 5th chordal degree may be used with any major chord at any time.. but the chord-scale relationship on those with diatonic roots will be less perfect.. and sound "farther out"

(Also note: Minor 7th chords are ocassionally tonic chords in disguise...so don't overlook the possibility of a non-diat. min 7th chord actually being a IIIm7 or VIm7 for I...see page 71.)

95

7th Position Study (duet)

Solo in G

Bb REAL MELODIC MINOR - 5 POSITIONS

FINGERING DERIVED
FROM TYPE 4

FROM TYPE 2

FROM TYPE 1A

FROM TYPE 3

FROM TYPE 1

fine

Chord Forms - 7th in the Bass

(* BASS (SOUNDING) RANGE.. FROM APPX. C (5th OR 6th STG'S) ON DOWN IN 'PITCH.

..CHORD VOICINGS WITH THE 7TH DEGREE IN THE BASS HAVE VERY WEAK
CHORDAL SOUNDS. THESE FORMS (LIKE THOSE WITH THE 3RD IN THE BASS)
MAY BE USED FOR INVERSION LEAPS OR AS "PASSING CHORDS"...BUT THEIR
USE MUST BE WELL JUSTIFIED (SUCH AS A STRONG DESCENDING BASS LINE)
OR THEY WILL SOUND WRONG.

Chord Etude No. 11

Two Octave Arpeggios — G MINOR TRIAD FROM THE 3rd

(Fingering derived from scales and chords-Across and up the fingerboard.)

(Practice all forms in all possible keys)

F MINOR TRIAD FROM THE 5th   (Across and up the fingerboard.)

(practice all forms in all possible keys)

KEY SIGNATURES the order of appearance of flats and sharps.

FLAT KEYS EVOLVE THRU-CYCLE 5
(DOWNWARD IN PERFECT FIFTHS)

SHARP KEYS EVOLVE THRU-NEGATIVE
CYCLE 5 (UPWARD IN PERF. FIFTHS)

Theory... Chord To Chord Motion

DESCRIPTIONS AND TERMS (A BRIEF DISCUSSION)

1.) Chord sequences (cadences) are represented by numerical terms or numbers that indicate the chords and their structures in the key of the moment. . . . If only a single number is used to represent a chord, the structure is assumed to be diatonic (in the indicated key). (i.e. two, five, one in C = Dm7 G7 C . . . two, five one in F = Gm7 C7 F)

2.) Non-diatonic structures are represented by two numbers, and (if necessary) a descriptive term or symbol...

EXAMPLES:

	one,	six-seven,	two-seven,	five,	one
	I	VI7	II7	V7	I
(KEY OF C)	C	A7	D7	G7	C

	one,	one sharp dim.,	two,	flat two-seven,	one
	I	I#°	IIm7	♭II7	I
(KEY OF C)	C	C#°	Dm7	D♭7	C

3.) Chord sequences are also described in another way. The word "cycle" followed by a number indicates the interval (distance) from chord root to chord root. In the most common chord progressions (cycle 5, cycle 3, cycle 7) the interval is figured downward. . . . Notice in the following examples that, in use, the direction of bass notes is optional . . . but the chords have been (in fact) constructed from the notes a 5th, 3rd, or 7th below.

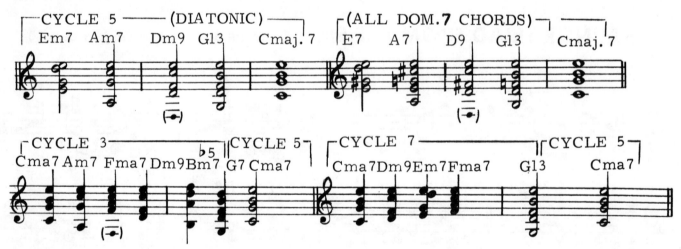

4.) When chord root motion goes up A 3rd, 5th, or 7th, it is called negative cycle 3, negative cycle 5, and negative cycle 7. (One sequence of 2 chords is common . . . further extension of negative cycles is less common.)

Both of the above methods of indicating chord motion are extremely valuable . . . especially in memorizing and transposing the chords to songs.

Example: (1st 16 bars)

I	VIm7	IIm7 V7	IIIm7	VI7	IIm7 V7	I	VIm7	II7	V7	I	♭III7	IIm7	♭II7
C	Am7	Dm7 G7	Em7	A7	Dm7 G7	C	Am7	D7	G7	C	E♭7	Dm7	D♭7

Bridge (or release)

CYCLE 5   (CONSTANT STRUCTURES)

III7 / E7	%	A7	%	D7	%	G7	%	Repeat 1st 8 measures

Chromatic Scale

The Chromatic Scale consists of 12 notes.... one half step apart.

FINGERING PATTERN 1

(ACROSS FINGERBOARD
NO POSITION CHANGE)

Examples of application show use of Chromatic Scales over augmented and diminished (optional dom 7(♭9)) chords. Observe use of sixteenth notes and triplets so that the first attack of each beat is a chord tone.

FINGERING PATTERN 2 Less practical than the fingering shown above, as the use of this pattern must be pre-set in order to come out in the proper position. (ACROSS-WITH POSITION CHANGES)

Eb REAL MELODIC MINOR - 5 POSITIONS

FINGERING DERIVED
FROM TYPE 3

FROM TYPE 1

FROM TYPE 4

FROM TYPE 2

(E♭ Mel. Min.)

FROM TYPE 1A

105

Chord Forms

Diminished 7th (with added high degrees)

Dim. 7th chords may be named from any chord tone. High degrees (2 frets above any dim. chord tone) give you the names of the four dom. 7 ♭9 chords with the same sound. (G°=A7♭9 B♭=C7♭9=D♭°=E♭7♭9=E°=F♯7♭9)

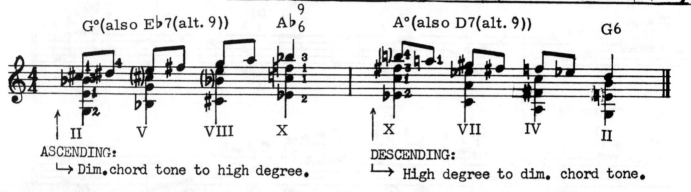

ASCENDING:
↳ Dim. chord tone to high degree.

DESCENDING:
↳ High degree to dim. chord tone.

Diminished 7th (with added high degrees)

High degrees on dim. 7th chords may also be thought of as the note one fret below any dim. chord tone (they will be the same four notes as those found 2 frets above.)

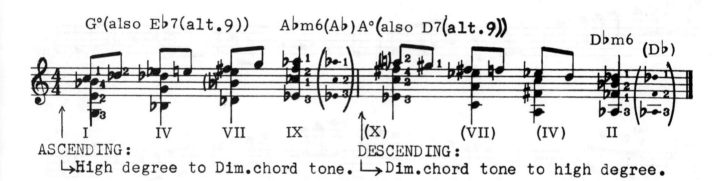

ASCENDING:
↳ High degree to Dim. chord tone.

DESCENDING:
↳ Dim. chord tone to high degree.

Chord Etude No. 12

Speed Study

TEMPO MUST BE CONSTANT THRU-OUT

(...FOR PRACTICE WITH OTHER FINGERING, CHANGE THE SIGNATURE TO C, F, D, AND A...ALSO USE SPEED STUDIES FOR REAL MELODIC MINOR SCALES...PRACTICE ALL SUGGESTED KEYS WITH ♭3.)

*Two Octave Arpeggios–*C DIMINISHED TRIAD FROM THE ROOT

(Across and up the fingerboard.)

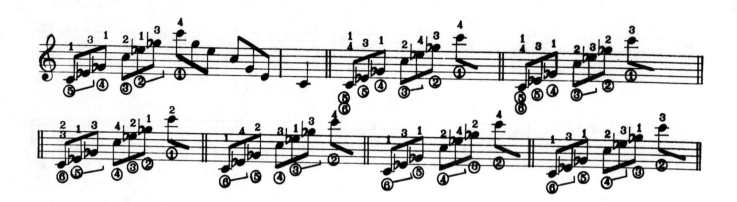

G DIMINISHED TRIAD FROM THE 3rd

F DIMINISHED TRIAD FROM THE 5th

(Practice all preceding dim. forms in all possible keys..)

Melodic Rhythm Study No. 7 (duet)

Whole Tone Scales - In Position

The Whole Tone Scale consists of 6 notes, a whole step apart. Each scale tone can be considered the tonic - therefore only 2 scales exist.

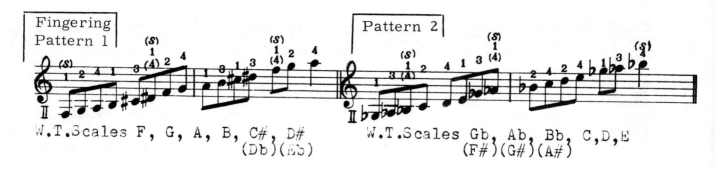

W.T.Scales F, G, A, B, C#, D#
(Db)(Eb)

W.T.Scales Gb, Ab, Bb, C, D, E
(F#)(G#)(A#)

Practice as follows: Ascending and descending from each finger. (First finger stretches are the most practical, but even eventually include all possibilities.)

(Memorize the fingering patterns...practice both W.T. Scales, in all positions)

Principal use of W. T. Scales in improvization is over augmented triads, and (aug.) Dom 7th's. (where the ninth is un-altered... or can be assumed to be un-altered.)

Examples:

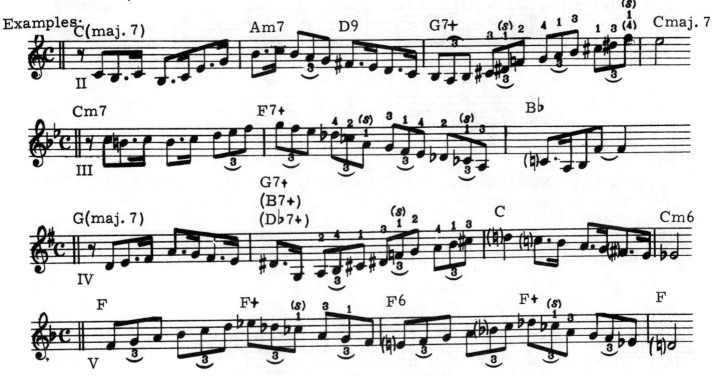

The following example employs both Whole Tone Scales..(same position).

ADDITIONAL WHOLE TONE SCALE FINGERINGS..WITH POSITION CHANGES

1.) Across and down the fingerboard as scale ascends(two octaves)

2.) constant fingering- position change every string (three octaves)

(These additional fingerings are less practical for general use.)

Rhythm Guitar - The Right Hand

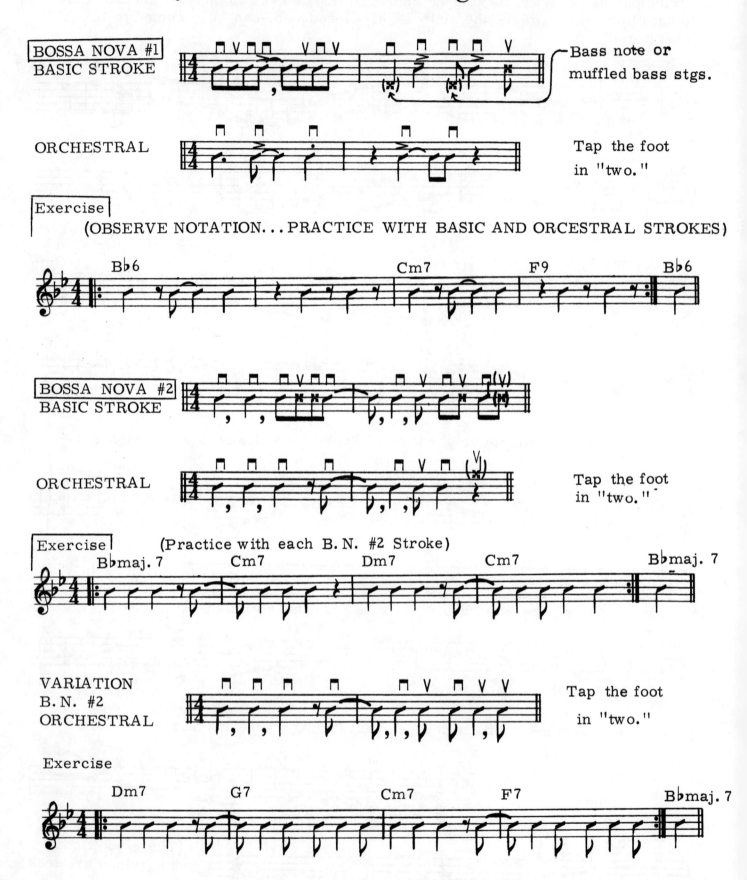

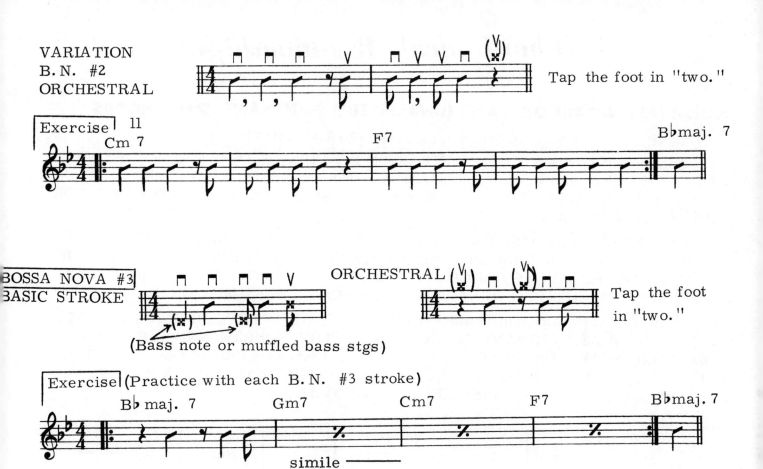

VARIATION
B. N. #2
ORCHESTRAL

Tap the foot in "two."

Exercise 11

Cm 7   F7   B♭maj. 7

BOSSA NOVA #3
BASIC STROKE

ORCHESTRAL

Tap the foot in "two."

(Bass note or muffled bass stgs)

Exercise (Practice with each B. N. #3 stroke)

B♭ maj. 7   Gm7   Cm7   F7   B♭maj. 7

simile ————

Two Octave Arpeggios— Bb, F# AND D AUGMENTED TRIADS

(...from the root, third and aug. 5th...Across and up the fingerboard.)

(...using the preceding forms practice and learn aug. triad arp's from all
notes possible..)

Chord - Scale Relationships

(FOR THE PURPOSE OF IMPROVISATION)

NON-DIATONIC MINOR 6 AND (UNALTERED*) DOMINANT 7th CHORDS

(*Unaltered in this instance means...No ♭9 +9 ♭5 or +5)

1.) THE TONIC AND SUBDOMINANT (I and IV) CHORDS IN A MAJOR KEY ARE OFTEN FOUND TEMPORARILY ALTERED TO MINOR 6th STRUCTURES.. (Im6 and IVm6). USE REAL MELODIC MIN SCALE BUILT FROM CHORD NAME FOR Im6 and IVm6 IN MAJ. KEY.

(..BE CAREFUL OF MIN 6th CHORDS.. BE SURE THEY ARE ACTUALLY FUNCTIONING AS Im6 OR IVm6 BEFORE EMPLOYING THE ABOVE. THEY ARE OFTEN MISNAMED MIN7♭5 CHORDS (THE DIATONIC VIIm7♭5 OF A MAJOR KEY) OR NINTH CHORDS (V7) RENAMED TO INDICATE BASS MOTION.)

2.) THESE SAME Im6 and IVm6 CHORDS WILL ALSO APPEAR (HARMONICALLY EXTENDED) AS DOMINANT 7th CHORDS ON THE FOURTH AND LOWERED SEVENTH SCALE DEGREES.. (IV7 and ♭VII7). (NOTE: THESE DOM 7th STRUCTURES INCLUDE CHORD DEGREES 9, 11+, 13) USE REAL MEL. MINOR SCALE FROM 5th CHORDAL DEGREE OF IV7 AND ♭VII7.

EXAMPLES:

CHORD -	C	Cm6	C	C7	F	Fm6	C G7	C
SCALE -	Cmaj	C Real Mel. Min.	Cmaj		Fmaj	C maj or Fmaj	F Real Mel. Min.	Cmaj ⟶

CHORD -	C	F9	C	C7	F	B♭9	C G7	C
SCALE -	(same as above)							

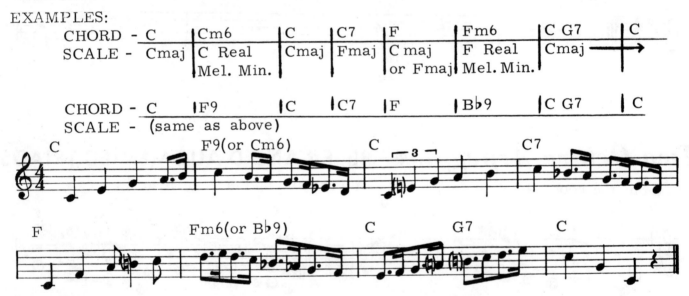

3.) ANY UNALTERED DOMINANT 7th CHORD WITH A NON-DIATONIC ROOT (NOT PRECEDED BY A MODULATING IIm7) WANTS TO SOUND LIKE ♭VII7.. OF WHATEVER KEY IT IS THE LOWERED SEVENTH DEGREE. (NOTE: ALL DOM 7 CHORDS WITH NON-DIAT. ROOTS INCLUDE CHORD DEGREES 9, 11+13) USE REAL MEL. MIN. SCALE FROM 5th CHORDAL DEGREE OF DOM7 WITH NON-DIAT. RT.

EXAMPLE:

CHORD -	C	E♭9	Am7	A♭13	Dm9	D♭9	C	B♭9	C
SCALE -	Cmaj	B♭ Real Mel. Min.	Cmaj	E♭ Real Mel. Min.	Cmaj	A♭ Real Mel. Min.	Cmaj	F Real Mel. Min.	Cma

4.) We do not (as yet) have the necessary "scale tools" to properly handle all dom 7th chords with diatonic roots. Therefore I suggest that (for now) you use the major or real mel. min. scale derived from the *intended tonic chord for all dom 7ths with scale tone roots..(except IV7...see preceding no. 2)

[* Intended tonic = where the chord would normally resolve.. B7 to [E], E7 to [A], A7 to [D], etc...]

(Note: Real melodic min. constructed from the 5th chordal degree may be used on any (unaltered) dom 7th at any time.. But, because most dom 7ths with scale tone roots have 9ths and/or 13ths altered by the surrounding key sound, this chord-scale relationship is imperfect. I recommend that you avoid this for now.)

* * * * * * * * *

You must hear the sound of related scales with chords. Have someone play the changes for you (or use a tape recorder) and experiment with them. Much depends upon your command of the scales..mentally and physically..and upon correct chord names.

It is a very long process to learn (well enuff' to use) the chord-scale relationships covering all harmonic situations. Only diligence, perseverance and considerable experimentation (including thinking, playing and listening) will eventually do it.

I have only "scratched the surface" in this book on chord and scale relationships....We will pursue this considerably further in Vol. III.

* * * * * * *

Solo In D

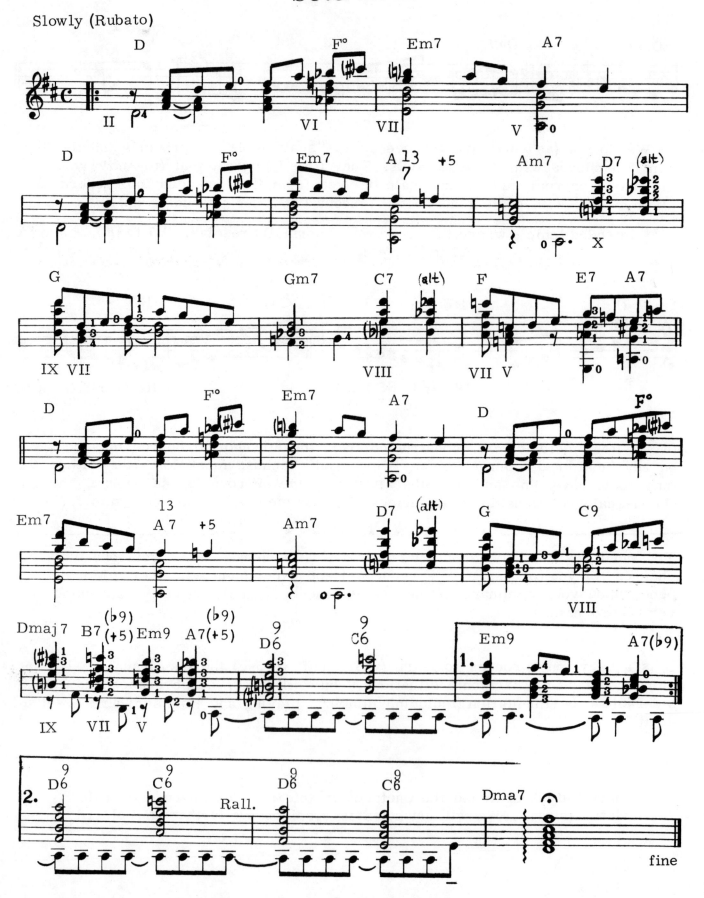

Index

MELODIC RHYTHM STUDIES (DUETS WITH SYNCOPATION)

RHYTHM GUITAR - THE RIGHT HAND

SCALES

SOLOS AND DUETS (ALSO SEE CHORD ETUDES AND MELODIC RHYTHM STUDIES)